MW01268666

PHARMACOLOGY
MNEMONICS

The Most Common Medication Prefixes, Suffixes, and Roots and How to Remember Them

Get a FREE set of Pharmacology Flashcards and be the first to know about NEW releases!

Visit Our Website

nursereadinessacademy.com

ISBN 9798393910983

DISCLAIMER

This book is intended as a reference guide for students, healthcare professionals, and others seeking information on pharmacology. The contents are based on the most current information available at the time of publication, and are intended to provide general information and educational material. This book is not intended to diagnose, treat, cure or prevent any disease or medical condition. If you have any health concerns, you should consult your healthcare professional. The information provided in this book is not intended to replace the advice of a qualified healthcare professional. If you are taking any medications, or have any medical conditions, you should consult your healthcare professional before starting any new treatment.

The authors and publishers make no representations or warranties with respect to the accuracy or completeness of the contents of this book and specifically disclaim any implied warranties of merchantability or fitness for a particular purpose. The authors and publishers shall not be held responsible for any errors or omissions, or for any damages resulting from the use of information contained in this book. This book is subject to change without notice, and the authors and publishers do not guarantee that any errors or omissions will be corrected. The information contained is intended for educational purposes only. By using this book, you agree to the terms of this disclaimer. If you do not agree with these terms, you should not use this book.

TABLE OF CONTENTS

Chapter 3: Steroids

Chapter 4: G.I.

Chapter 5: Psych/CNS

Chapter 6: Respiratory

Chapter 7: Anti-Inflammatory

Chapter 8: Diuretics

Chapter 9: Antiviral

Chapter 10: Cancer Drugs

Chapter 11: Miscellaneous

FROM THE AUTHOR

Pharmacology Mnemonics is my attempt to offer a practical approach to organizing and remembering the vast array of drug names you will encounter in your career.

Medicine is a complex field filled with countless medications, each with its own intricacies. Memorizing them all can be overwhelming. But don't worry! This book offers a solution—a method of categorization that simplifies the process.

By identifying common prefixes, suffixes, and roots in generic drug names, we can break them down into manageable 'chunks'. These chunks serve as building blocks, allowing us to recognize patterns and make connections between medications and their respective classes.

To further cement this information in your mind, I have created memory devices to go along with each prefix, suffix, and root. Just as "Please Excuse My Dear Aunt Sally" guided many through math class, I have applied the art (and science) of mnemonics to help solidify your knowledge of medications. In addition, space has been provided for the creation of your own memory devices. Oftentimes the sillier and more outlandish your memory device, the more effective it is. So have some fun with it!

It is my hope that by the end of this book you will have a practical framework to organize and recall medications, as well as the tools to successfully navigate the new information you will no doubt encounter as you progress in your career. Here's to a better way to study pharmacology, with *Pharmacology Mnemonics*!

Happy Studying!

Taylor
Founder, Nurse Readiness Academy

CHAPTER 1: CARDIOVASCULAR

-AFIL

Amplify a Fellow's Impaired Longjohn

Class:
Phosphodiesterase (PDE) Inhibitor

Indications:
Chronic Obstructive Pulmonary Disease (COPD), Erectile Dysfunction (ED), Pulmonary Arterial Hypertension (PAH)

Generic Names:
avan<u>afil</u>, silden<u>afil</u>, tadal<u>afil</u>, varden<u>afil</u>

A	Amplify a
F	Fellow's
I	Impaired
L	Longjohn

-DIPINE

DIP IN Extra calcium

Class:
Calcium Channel Blocker

Indications:
Hypertension, Congestive Heart Failure (CHF), Coronary Artery Spasm, Acute Coronary Syndrome

Generic Names:
amlo<u>dipine</u>, felo<u>dipine</u>, nife<u>dipine</u>, nimo<u>dipine</u>

D	Dip
I	
P	
I	In
N	
E	Extra calcium

-OLOL

Optimally Lower Olga's Lionheart

Class:

Beta Blocker

Indications:

Hypertension, Congestive Heart Failure (CHF), Coronary Artery Disease, Tachycardias

Generic Names:

aten<u>olol</u>, metopr<u>olol</u>, nad<u>olol</u>, propran<u>olol</u>, tim<u>olol</u>

O	Optimally
L	Lower
O	Olga's
L	Lionheart

PARIN, -PARIN

Prevent Any Restiction IN blood flow

Class:

Antithrombotic / Anticoagulant

Indications:

Prophylaxis for Deep Vein Thrombosis (DVT) and Pulmonary Embolism (PE), Atrial Fibrillation (A-Fib)

Generic Names:

heparin, enoxaparin, dalteparin, fondaparinux

P	Prevent
A	Any
R	Restriction
I	In blood flow
N	

-PRIL

Prepare **R**AAS **I**nhibition, **L**ower BP

Class:
ACE Inhibitor

Indications:
Hypertension, Congestive Heart Failure (CHF), Acute
Myocardial Infarction (AMI)

Generic Names:
benaze<u>pril</u>, capto<u>pril</u>, enala<u>pril</u>, lisino<u>pril</u>, moexi<u>pril</u>,
rami<u>pril</u>

P	Prepare
R	RAAS
I	Inhibition
L	Lower BP

-SARTAN

Stay Away Renin! This Angiotensin's Nixed

Class:

Angiotensin II Receptor Antagonist (ARB)

Indications:

Hypertension, Diabetic Neuropathy, Congetsive Heart Failure (CHF)

Generic Names:

cande_sartan_, irbe_sartan_, lo_sartan_, olme_sartan_, val_sartan_

S	Stay
A	Away
R	Renin
T	This
A	Angiotension's
N	Nixed

-STATIN

STAy Trim! Inhibit Nachos

Class:

HMG-CoA Reductase Inhibitor / Statins

Indications:

Hyperlipidemia, Prophylaxis for Myocardial Infarction and Stroke

Generic Names:

atorvastatin, lovastatin, pitavastatin, pravastatin, rosuvastatin, simvastatin

STA Sounds Like STAY

S	Stay
T	
A	
T	Trim
I	Inhibit
N	Nachos

-ZOSIN

Zap Overactive Sympathetic Innervation Now

Class:
Alpha Blocker

Indications:
Hypertension, Congestive Heart Failure (CHF), Benign Prostatic Hyperplasia (BPH), Nephrolithiasis

Generic Names:
alfuzosin, doxazosin, prazosin, terazosin

Z	Zap
O	Overactive
S	Sympathetic
I	Innervation
N	Now

CHAPTER 2:
ANTIMICROBIALS

CEF- / CEPH-

Cure **E**ven **F**requent infections

Class:
Cephalosporin Antibiotic

Indications:
Urinary Tract Infection (UTI), Otitis Media, Tonsillitis, Gonorrhea

Generic Names:
cefaclor, cefdinir, cefixime, cefprozil, cephalexin

C	Cure
E	Even
F	Frequent infections

-CILLIN

Penicillins are ChILLIN'

Class:
Penicillin Antibiotic

Indications:
Pneumonia, Dental Abscess, and other Bacterial Infections Caused by Gram-Positive Bacteria

Generic Names:
amoxi<u>cillin</u>, ampi<u>cillin</u>, dicloxa<u>cillin</u>, af<u>cillin</u>, oxa<u>cillin</u>

PENICILLINS are

Ch	
I	
L	
L	
I	
N'	

-CYCLINE

CYCLe microbes INto Extinction

Class:
Tetracycline Antibiotic

Indications:
Cellulitis, Skin Abscess, Necrotising Infections, Diabetic Foot Ulcers

Generic Names:
demeclocycline, doxycycline, minocycline, tetracycline

C	Cycle microbes
Y	
C	
L	
I	Into
N	
E	Extinction

-DAZOLE

DAYS Over for Lazy Enterococci

Class:
Anthelmintic / Antibiotic

Indications:
Bacterial Vaginosis, Pelvic Inflammatory Disease (PID), Gum Disease, Rosacea

Generic Names:
albendazole, mebendazole, metronidazole, tinidazole

DAZ sounds like DAYS

D	Days
A	
Z	
O	Over for
L	Lazy
E	Enterococci

-FLOXACIN

FLEX on **A**ny **C**hallenging **I**nfections, **N**erd

Class:
Quinolone Antibiotic

Indications:
Community Acquired Pneumonia, Acute Bacterial
Exacerbation of Chronic Bronchitis, Bacterial Sinusitis

Generic Names:
besifloxacin, ciprofloxacin, levofloxacin,
moxifloxacin, olfloxacin

FLOX sounds like FLEX

F	Flex on
L	
O	
X	
A	Any
C	Challenging
I	Infections
N	Nerd

-MYCIN

Mycobacteria, **Y**ou **C**an't **I**gnore myci**N**'s might!

Class:

Antibiotic

Indications:

Community Acquired Pneumonia, Bacterial Sinusitis, Acute Bacterial Exacerbations of Chronic Obstructive Pulmonary Disease (COPD)

Generic Names:

azithro<u>mycin</u>, clarithro<u>mycin</u>, clinda<u>mycin</u>, erythro<u>mycin</u>

	M	Mycobacteria
	Y	You
	C	Can't
	I	Ignore
myciN	N	's might!

-NAZOLE

Nix Athlete's Zesty Odor and Live Easy

Class:
Antifungal

Indications:
Candidiasis / Thrush, Urinary Tract Infection (UTI), Peritonitis

Generic Names:
fluconazole, ketoconazole, miconazole, terconazole, tioconazole

N	Nix
A	Athlete's
Z	Zesty
O	Odor and
L	Live
E	Easy

SULFA-

Slay Unfriendly Little Fiends with Antibiotics

Class:

Antibiotic

Indications:

Pneumonia, Otitis Media, Urinary Tract Infection (UTI), Traveler's Diarrhea, Acute Bacteria Exacerbations of Chronic Bronchitis

Generic Names:

sulfacetamide, sulfadiazine, sulfamethoxazole, sulfasalazine

S	Slay
U	Unfriendly
L	Little
F	Fiends with
A	Antibiotics

CHAPTER 3:
STEROIDS

-ASONE

All Swollen? Oh No! Ease up

Class:

Corticosteroid

Indications:

Allergic Reactions, Asthma, Adrenal Insufficiency, Cerebral Edema, Acute Respiratory Distress Syndrome (ARDS)

Generic Names:

betamethasone, dexamethasone, diflorasone, fluticasone, mometasone

A	All
S	Swollen?
O	Oh
N	No!
E	Ease up

CORT

Cortisol Opposes Relaxation Time

Class:
Corticosteroid

Indications:
Inflammation, Status Asthmaticus, Adrenal Insufficiency, Physiologic Replacement (Pediatrics)

Generic Names:
clocortolone, fludrocortisone, hydrocortisone

C	Cortisol
O	Opposes
R	Relazation
T	Time

-OLONE

OnLy ONE medication for your inflammation

Class:
Corticosteroid

Indications:
Asthma, Angioedema, Bells Palsy, Adrenal Insufficiency, Chronic Obstructive Pulmonary Disease (COPD), Gout, Hepatitis, Inflammatory Bowel Disease (IBD), Systemic Rheumatic Disorders

Generic Names:
fluocin<u>olone</u>, fluorometh<u>olone</u>, prednis<u>olone</u>, triamcin<u>olone</u>

O	Only
L	
O	One medication for your inflammation
N	
E	

-OLONE *

Out Lift anyONE

Class:
Anabolic Steroid

Indication:
Anemia, Osteoporosis, Burns, Radiation Therapy, Surgery, Trauma

Generic Names:
nandr<u>olone</u>, oxandr<u>olone</u>, oxymeth<u>olone</u>

O	Out
L	Lift any
O	One
N	
E	

-ONIDE

Once Nerves are Inflamed, Don't Endure it

Class:

Corticosteroid

Indications:

Dermatitis, Eczema, Psoriasis, Allergic Rash

Generic Names:

budes<u>onide</u>, cicles<u>onide</u>, des<u>onide</u>, fluocin<u>onide</u>, halcin<u>onide</u>

O	Once
N	Nerves are
I	Inflamed
D	Don't
E	Endure it

PRED- / PRED

PREDictably defeat **RED**ness and **ED**ema

Class:

Corticosteroid

Indications:

Asthma, Angioedema, Bells Palsy, Adrenal Insufficiency, Chronic Obstructive Pulmonary Disease (COPD), Gout, Hepatitis, Inflammatory Bowel Disease (IBD), Systemic Rheumatic Disorders

Generic Names:

lote**pred**nol, **pred**nicarbate, **pred**nisolone, **pred**nisone

P	Predictably defeat
R	Redness and
E	Edema
D	

CHAPTER 4:
G.I.

-EPRAZOLE

Enjoy Pizza, Reduce Acid, SOUL food's great!

Class:
Proton Pump Inhibitor (PPI)

Indications:
Heartburn, Indigestion, Gastroesophageal Reflux Disease (GERD), Ulcers (Peptic, Duodenal, Gastric)

Generic:
esom<u>eprazole</u>, om<u>eprazole</u>, rab<u>eprazole</u>

ZOLE sounds like SOUL

E	Enjoy
P	Pizza
R	Reduce
A	Acid
Z	Soul food's great!
O	
L	
E	

-NACIN

No Accidents, Cure Incontinence Now

Class:
Muscarinic Antagonist (Anticholinergic)

Indications:
Urinary Incontinence, Overactive Bladder, Urinary Frequency and Urgency

Generic:
darife<u>nacin</u>, solife<u>nacin</u>

N	No
A	Accidents
C	Cure
I	Incontinence
N	Now

-OPRAZOLE

Oh Please Reduce Acid, poZOLE tastes great!

Class:
Proton Pump Inhibitor (PPI)

Indications:
Heartburn, Indigestion, Gastroesophageal Reflux Disease (GERD), Ulcers (Peptic, Duodenal, Gastric)

Generic Names:
dexlansoprazole, lansoprazole, pantoprazole

O	Oh
P	Please
R	Reduce
A	Acid
Z	poZOLE tastes great!
O	
L	
E	

-SETRON

Suppress Emesis Today, Ride On Nausea-free

Class:
Antiemetic

Indications:
Prevention of Nausea and Vomiting

Generic Names:
dolasetron, granisetron, ondansetron, palonosetron

S	Suppress
E	Emesis
T	Today
R	Ride
O	On
N	Nausea-free

CHAPTER 5:
PSYCH/CNS

-BITAL

Bask In The Awesome Lull

Class:

Barbiturate / Sedative

Indications:

Seizures, Elevated Intracranial Pressure (ICP), Insomnia, Pre-Anesthetic

Generic Names:

butabar<u>bital</u>, butal<u>bital</u>, phenobar<u>bital</u>, secobar<u>bital</u>

B	Bask
I	In
T	The
A	Awesome
L	Lull

-PRAMINE

PRAy happiness will be **MINE**

Class:

Tricyclic Antidepressant (TCA)

Indications:

Depression, Anxiety, Cataplexy Syndrome, Insomnia, Neuropathic Pain, Body Dysmorphic Disorder, Panic Disorder

Generic Names:

clomi*pramine*, desi*pramine*, imi*pramine*, trimi*pramine*

PRA sounds like PRAY

P	Pray happiness will be
R	
A	
M	Mine
I	
N	
E	

-RIDONE

Get **RID Of N**ever **E**nding psychosis

Class:
Atypical Antipsychotic

Indications:
Schizophrenia, Bipolar I Acute Manic or Mixed Episodes, Autism-associated Irritability

Generic Names:
iloperidone, paliperidone, risperidone

	Get
R	Rid
I	
D	
O	Of
N	Never
E	Ending psychosis

-TRIPTAN

Vacation **TRIP**s make you relaxed and **TAN**

Class:
Selective 5-HT Receptor Agonist / Antimigraine

Indications:
Migraine Headaches

Generic Names:
almo<u>triptan</u>, ele<u>triptan</u>, riza<u>triptan</u>, suma<u>triptan</u>, zolmi<u>triptan</u>

	Vacation
T	Trips make you relaxed and
R	
I	
P	
T	Tan
A	
N	

-TYLINE

Take **Y**our **L**ife **I**n **N**ew **E**uphoric directions

Class:
Tricyclic Antidepressants (TCA)

Indications:
Depression, Anxiety, Post-Traumatic Stress Disorder (PTSD), Insomnia, Chronic Pain

Generic Names:
amitrip<u>tyline</u>, nortrip<u>tyline</u>, protrip<u>tyline</u>

T	Take
Y	Your
L	Life
I	In
N	New
E	Euphoric directions

-ZEPAM

Zebras Eat Popcorn And Mellow out

Class:
Benzodiazepine

Indications:
Anxiety Disorders, Alcohol Detoxification, Recurrent Seizures, Muscle Spasms

Generic Names:
clonazepam, diazepam, flurazepam, lorazepam, temazepam

Z	Zebras
E	Eat
P	Popcorn
A	And
M	Mellow out

-ZODONE

Zap Out Depression **ONE** dose at a time

Class:

Serotonin Antagonist and Re-Uptake Inhibitor /
Antidepressant

Indications:

Major Depressive Disorder (MDD)

Generic Names:

nefa<u>zodone</u>, tra<u>zodone</u>, vila<u>zodone</u>

Z	Zap
O	Out
D	Depression
O	One dose at a time
N	
E	

-ZOLAM

Zany Otters Laughing, Anxiety Melts

Class:
Benzodiazepine

Indications:
Peri-Operative Sedation/Anxiolysis/Amnesia, Acute Seizures

Generic Names:
alpra<u>zolam</u>, esta<u>zolam</u>, mida<u>zolam</u>, tria<u>zolam</u>

Z	Zany
O	Otters
L	Laughing
A	Anxiety
M	Melts

CHAPTER 6:
RESPIRATORY

-PHYLLINE

Puff, Hold Your Lungs in LINE

Class:
Xanthine Derivative / Bronchodilator

Indications:
Asthma, Chronic Bronchitis, Emphysema, COPD

Generic Names:
aminophylline, dyphylline, oxtriphylline, theophylline

P	Puff
H	Hold
Y	Your
L	Lungs in
L	Line
I	
N	
E	

-TEROL

Take it **E**asy, **R**elax, **O**pen **L**ungs

Class:

Beta Agonist / Bronchodilator

Indications:

Acute Bronchospasm, Asthma, Bronchitis, Emphysema, COPD

Generic Names:

albu<u>terol</u>, arformo<u>terol</u>, formo<u>terol</u>, levalbu<u>terol</u>, salme<u>terol</u>

T	Take it
E	Easy
R	Relax
O	Open
L	Lungs

CHAPTER 7:
ANTI-INFLAMMATORY

-FENAC

Forget Every Nagging AChe!

Class:

Non-Steroidal Anti-Inflammatory Drug (NSAID)

Indications:

Generalized Pain and Inflammation, Migraines, Osteoarthritis, Dysmenorrhea, Rheumatoid Arthritis

Generic Names:

bromfenac, diclofenac, nepafenac

F	Forget
E	Every
N	Nagging
A	Ache
C	

-IRAMINE

Ichy **R**ashes? **A**llergies? **MINE** no more

Class:
Antihistamine

Indications:
Allergy, Angioedema, Asthma, Conjunctivitis, Dermatitis, Eczema, Hay Fever, Rhinitis, Urticaria

Generic Names:
brompheniramine, chlorpheniramine, pheniramine

I	Itchy
R	Rashes
A	Allergies
M	Mine no more
I	
N	
E	

-MAB

Make Antibodies Ballistic

Class:
Monoclonal Antibody

Indications:
Crohn's Disease, Ulcerative Colitis, Rheumatoid Arthritis, Ankylosing Spondylitis, Psoriatic Arthritis, Plaque Psoriasis

Generic Names:
adalimumab, daclizumab, infliximab, omalizumab, trastuzumab

M	Make
A	Antibodies
B	Ballistic

-PROFEN

PRO Footballers want **E**asy k**N**ees

Class:
Non-Steroidal Anti-Inflammatory Drug (NSAID)

Indications:
Headache, Dental Pain, Menstrual Cramps, Muscle Aches, Arthritis

Generic Names:
feno<u>profen</u>, flurbi<u>profen</u>, ibu<u>profen</u>, keto<u>profen</u>

P	Pro
R	
O	
F	Footballers want
E	Easy
N	kNees

-TADINE

This Allergy Defense Inhibits Nasal Eruptions

Class:

Antihistamine

Indications:

Allergy, Angioedema, Asthma, Conjunctivitis, Dermatitis, Eczema, Hay Fever, Rhinitis, Urticaria

Generic Names:

cyprohep<u>tadine</u>, deslora<u>tadine</u>, lora<u>tadine</u>, olopa<u>tadine</u>

T	This
A	Allergy
D	Defense
I	Inhibits
N	Nasal
E	Eruptions

CHAPTER 8: DIURETICS

-LAMIDE

LA smog Makes Itchy Dry Eyes

Class:

Carbonic Anhydrase Inhibitor

Indications:

Glaucoma, Idiopathic Intracranial Hypertension, Congestive Heart Failure, Altitude Sickness

Generic Names:

acetazolamide, brinzolamide, dorzolamide, methazolamide

L	LA smog
A	
M	Makes
I	Itchy
D	Dry
E	Eyes

-SEMIDE

See Edema Melt In Diuresis Escape

Class:
Loop Diuretic

Indications:
Congestive Heart Failure (CHF), Cirrhosis of the Liver, Renal Disease / Nephrotic Syndrome

Generic Names:
furosemide, torsemide

S	See
E	Edema
M	Melt
I	In
D	Diuresis
E	Escape

-THIAZIDE

Take Heart In A Zippy Diuresis, Excrete!

Class:

Thiazide Diuretic

Indications:

Congestive Heart Failure (CHF), Hepatic Cirrhosis, Renal Dysfunction, Hypertension

Generic Names:

chloro<u>thiazide</u>, hydrochloro<u>thiazide</u>, methyclo<u>thiazide</u>

T	Take
H	Heart
I	In
A	A
Z	Zippy
D	Diuresis
E	Excrete

CHAPTER 9: ANTIVIRAL

-TADINE*

Totally Annihilates DNA In Nasty Epidemics

Class:
Antiviral (Influenza A)

Indications:
Prophylaxis and Treatment of Various Strains of Influenza A

Generic Names:
amantadine, rimantadine

T	Totally
A	Annihilates
D	DNA
I	In
N	Nasty
E	Epidemics

VIR, -VIR

Viciously **I**nhibit **R**eplication of HIV

Class:
Antiviral (HIV)

Indications:
Treatment of HIV-1 Infection

Generic Names:
abaca<u>vir</u>, efa<u>vir</u>enz, enfu<u>vir</u>tide, ne<u>vir</u>apine, ritona<u>vir</u>, tenofo<u>vir</u>

V	Viciously
I	Inhibit
R	Replication of HIV

VIR, -VIR*

Vanquish Infection, Repair the liver

Class:

Antiviral (Hepatitis)

Indications:

Treatment Hepatitis

Generic Names:

adefo<u>vir</u>, enteca<u>vir</u>, riba<u>vir</u>in

V	Vanquish
I	Infection
R	Repair the liver

-VIR

Va-va-vroom Infection Retreats, ramp up
your sex feats!

Class:
Antiviral (Herpes)

Indications:
Herpes Zoster, Genital Herpes, Chickenpox

Generic Names:
acyclo<u>vir</u>, famciclo<u>vir</u>, penciclo<u>vir</u>, valacyclo<u>vir</u>

V	Va-va-vroom
I	Infection
R	Retreats, ramp up your sex feats

-VIR*

C'Mon! Stop this VIRulent takeover!

Class:
Antiviral (CMV)

Indications:
Treatment of Cytomegaloviral Retinitis (CMV)

Generic Names:
cidofo<u>vir</u>, ganciclo<u>vir</u>, valganciclo<u>vir</u>

C'Mon to remember CMV

	stop this
V	Virulent takeover
I	
R	

-VIR**

Vanquish Influenza Rapidly

Class:
Antiviral (Influenza A and B)

Indications:
Treatment of Influenza A and B

Generic Names:
oseltami<u>vir</u>, zanami<u>vir</u>

V	Vanquish
I	Influenza
R	Rapidly

-VUDINE

Virus Undefeated? Deploy Instant
Nucleoside Execution

Class:
Antiviral Nucleoside Analogue

Indications:
Treatment of HIV and HBV

Generic Names:
lami<u>vudine</u>, sta<u>vudine</u>, telbi<u>vudine</u>, zido<u>vudine</u>

V	Virus
U	Undefeated
D	Deploy
I	Instant
N	Nucleoside
E	Execution

CHAPTER 10:
CANCER DRUGS

-BICIN

Bye bye **C**ancer, **I**t's **N**ixed!

Class:
Antineoplastic / Cytotoxic Agent

Indications:
Treatment of Various Forms of Cancer Including
Leukemia, Lymphoma, Breast Cancer, Bladder Cancer,
Neuroblastoma, Ovarian Cancer, and Thyroid Cancer

Generic Names:
doxoru<u>bicin</u>, epiru<u>bicin</u>, idaru<u>bicin</u>, valru<u>bicin</u>

BYE sounds like BI

B	Bye, bye
I	
C	Cancer
I	It's
N	Nixed

-MUSTINE

MUSTY Neoplasms

Class:
Antineoplastic / Alkalating Agent

Indications:
Brain Tumors, Prostate Cancer, Non-Hodgkin Lymphoma

Generic Names:
carmustine, estramustine, lomustine, bendamustine

MUSTY sounds like MUSTI

M	Musty
U	
S	
T	
I	
N	Neoplasms
E	

-TINIB

Tame Illness Now, I Beat cancer

Class:
Antineoplastic / Kinase Inhibitor

Indications:
Metastatic Non-Small Cell Lung Cancer (NSCLC), Chronic Myeloid Leukemia (CML)

Generic Names:
crizotinib, dasatinib, erlotinib, gefitinib, imatinib

T	Tame
I	Illness
N	Now
I	I
B	Beat cancer

CHAPTER 11: MISCELLANEOUS

-CAINE

No pain, all gain with **CAINE**

Class:

Local Anesthetic

Indications:

Local and Topical Anesthesia

Generic Names:

bupiva<u>caine</u>, lido<u>caine</u>, mepiva<u>caine</u>, prilo<u>caine</u>, propara<u>caine</u>

	No Pain, All Gain with
C	
A	
I	
N	
E	

-DRONATE

Don't **R**eabsorb **O**ur **N**ew lun**ATE**

Class:
Bisphosphonate / Bone Resorption Inhibitor

Indications:
Osteoporosis, Paget's Disease, Hypercalcemia

Generic Names:
alen<u>dronate</u>, eti<u>dronate</u>, iban<u>dronate</u>, rise<u>dronate</u>

D	Don't
R	Reabsorb
O	Our
N	New
lun ATE	

-GLIPTIN

Drink more Lipton with **GLIPTIN**

Class:
Antidiabetic / DPP-4 Enzyme Inhibitor

Indications:
Management of Type 2 Diabetes Mellitus

Generic Names:
saxagliptin, sitagliptin, linagliptin

LIPTON rhymes with GLIPTIN

	Drink More Lipton With
G	
L	
I	
P	
T	
I	
N	

-GLITAZONE

All that **GLITAZ** is glucose

Class:
Antidiabetic / Thiazolidinedione

Indications:
Management of Type 2 Diabetes Mellitus

Generic Names:
pioglitazone, rosiglitazone, troglitazone

GLITAZ sounds like GLITTERS

	All That
G	
L	
I	
T	
A	
Z	is glucose
O	
N	
E	

-TREL

Tame and Regulate Estrogen Levels

Class:
Progestin / Female Hormone

Indications:
Prevention of Pregnancy

Generic Names:
desogestrel, etonogestrel, levonorgestrel, norgestrel

T	Tame and
R	Regulate
E	Estrogen
L	Levels

TRETIN-, TRETIN, -TRETIN

Tackling Rough Epidermis? Try It Now!

Class:
Retinoid / Dermatologic Agent (Vitamin A)

Indications:
Psoriasis, Severe Acne, Wrinkle Reduction

Generic Names:
acitretin, alitretinoin, isotretinoin, tretinoin

T	Tackling
R	Rough
E	Epidermis
T	Try
I	It
N	Now